Don't Get Off the Train

En Route to Your Divine Destination

YOU MAY ORDER FROM:
THE CHRISTIAN GOLDMINE
87 Kight Circle
LaGrange, GA 30240
706/882-7069
Fax: 706/882-7001
Email: JonesHL@AOL.COM

Juanita Bynum

Pneuma Life

PUBLISHING

Don't Get Off the Train

Printed in the United States of America
ISBN: 1-56229-121-1

Pneuma Life Publishing
Post Office Box 885
Lanham, MD 20703-0885
(301) 577-4052

Visit our webpage at http://www.pneumalife.com

4   5 6 7 8 Printing/Year 04 03 02 01 00 99

Contents

Acknowledgments
Dedication
Preface
Introduction

Chapter   Page

Acknowledgments

First to my Lord and Savior Jesus Christ, Who is the author and finisher of my faith; I would like to thank my parents, Mr. and Mrs. Thomas Bynum who were so instrumental in helping me to the next level in God. To John and Valerie Boyd, thanks for being true friends. And to the staff of Juanita Bynum Ministries: *"Don't Get Off the Train!"*

Dedication

This book is dedicated to Pastor and Sister William T. Nichols who were so instrumental in getting me on the train. I would also like to dedicate this book to Mother Katherine Lott and Evangelist Margaret Hill.

Don't Get Off the Train

Preface

Why must I tell my story?

I must tell it for the same reason the Bible was written–that others may live. Every story in the Bible stands as a perpetual statute telling us that we can make it.

I did!

Others have!

You will!

Have you ever been caught in your most embarrassing moment? Do we have anything in common with the woman caught in the very act of adultery?

Yes.

We started clean. We ended dirty. Everybody saw it, and Jesus covered us.

Some lives stand out more than others. Some are chosen to proclaim, "I did it, but I recovered–and so will you. I've been healed, and you can be healed too. I made it, and you're going to make it–if you don't get off the train!"

There are things that only certain people can do.

Only a Samuel or Elijah can express the heart of a prophet. Only a David can reach a fallen king. Only a woman at the well can minister to a woman who slept with many.

Only a little boy who gave his two fish and five loaves of bread knows what it means to sacrifice a lunch. He can tell you the importance of giving up something for the sake of others. Only a Peter can minister to someone who denies that he knows the Lord yet has God's call upon his life. Only a Paul can help you understand what it's like to be blind, transformed, and renewed after breathing threats of murder. Only a Hosea can marry a woman who has been with other men and yet show the meaning of true love.

This is precisely my story. Only Juanita Bynum can do certain things. God has given me certain people to touch in ministry. I can only minister what I have been through. That's why I can minister to you. I've been there.

Read on with an open heart and be encouraged. No matter where you've been or what you've been through, let God touch you deeply. Remember that you can only give away what you have. Once you've been saved, healed, and delivered, you become a choice instrument who can effectively minister to those in need.

Introduction

Where Do We Go From Here?

With the glory of the Lord falling all across the country, many people are asking, "Lord, where do we go from here?" The Lord gave me a resounding answer to this question. He said, "Juanita, My people must go higher and deeper."

We have not even scratched the surface of where God's going to take those of us who are willing to go somewhere. You will not be able to convince people where God is taking us because their finite, carnal minds cannot comprehend the length and the breadth of what God is doing.

> But the natural man receiveth not the things of the Spirit of God: for they are foolishness unto him: neither can he know them, because they are spiritually discerned (1 Corinthians 2:14).

The natural mind cannot comprehend the things of the Spirit. That's why you can't explain God to the flesh.

Your Flesh Has One Job

We were born and wrapped in flesh for one purpose. The flesh was created to house the anointing. If the people of God would recognize that we do not owe flesh an explanation, we would begin to walk in the liberty that Jesus purchased for us. My flesh has one job and one job only–to house the Spirit of God that man may see God through the flesh.

For many people, the flesh is God. They answer to the flesh. They respond to the flesh. They even worship the flesh. We are all out of control in the flesh. We can't allow the flesh to rule us because it is the enemy of God.

> For to be carnally minded is death; but to be spiritually minded is life and peace. Because the carnal mind is enmity against God: for it is not subject to the law of God, neither indeed can be. So then they that are in the flesh cannot please God. But ye are not in the flesh, but in the Spirit, if so be that the Spirit of God dwell in you (Romans 8:6-9a).

Do you know what this means?

The flesh doesn't own me. It doesn't dictate to me; it doesn't tell me when to praise God and when not to praise God. It doesn't hinder me; it doesn't get in my way. It has only one job–to provide a house for the Spirit of God.

Who's in Control?

Many of us can't praise God because our flesh is in control. We don't seem to know the purpose of flesh, but as the song says, "When I think of the goodness of Jesus and all that He's done for me, my soul–not my flesh–cries out, 'Hallelujah!'"

> Bless the Lord, O my *soul:* and all that is within me, bless his holy name. Bless the Lord, O my *soul,* and forget not all his benefits (Psalm 103:1,2).

David told us exactly what part of him would bless the Lord. He didn't say that his flesh would bless the Lord, but he did say his soul would. Because he knew the purpose of the flesh, David refused to let it prohibit his praise.

I want to live like David. No matter what I'm going through, my soul cries out to God. No matter what the devil says to my flesh on the outside, my soul praises God from the inside, "Hallelujah! Thank God for saving me!"

Someone may ask, "How can you praise God in the midst of what you're going through?" My soul–not my flesh–is in control.

Sometimes we just don't feel like praising the Lord. We sit in church and focus on our problems. Suddenly, in the midst of our pain and agony, our hands go up. We often don't understand this quickening in our spirit. The explanation is simple. Your spirit took control of your flesh, commanding praise to emerge.

> I will bless the Lord at all times: his praise shall continually be in my mouth. My soul shall make her boast in the Lord: the humble shall hear thereof, and be glad. O magnify the Lord with me, and let us exalt his name together (Psalm 34:1-3).

David said he would bless the Lord at *all* times. That means in the good times as well as the bad. That verse is powerful. David was in control of his flesh. Regardless of the situation, even when he could have complained, David commended his God. His mouth would not be filled with disgust and negativity but worship and praise. David realized that if he continually proclaimed God's goodness, the Spirit of God would begin to fill the space that misery had occupied. In essence, there would be no room for the devil's junk. The glory of the Lord would fill him.

If the glory of the Lord is on the inside, it will shine forth on the outside. The glory draws people. That's why David said, "O magnify the Lord with me." The glory of the Lord draws others. As people draw closer to the glory, the glory draws closer to them, and there is no room for the devil to get between.

In this next move of the Spirit, God is going to get so close to His people. Things that used to get in the way won't fit anymore. We're getting ready to be pressed beyond measure. We're going to be compressed and compacted, and the flesh will be mashed out of us.

Unless you understand the experience of the wine press, you will not understand what it means to be mashed out. If we want to get the Spirit of God inside and to get the anointing out, we must be pressed beyond measure. This won't be a popular teaching. Some people shun difficulty and suffering.

Thank You, Jesus. You chose not to go the easy route. Thank You, because the pain is great and the pressure is hard. There's a reward in it, but it's not in this life. I'm not moved by what I see, and I don't operate on what I feel. I don't allow God to use me based on my circumstances because I've tapped into another realm.

Listen to the Conductor

A Conductor is in charge of our lives. He monitors our every move. He knows when we've gotten off at the wrong stop and signed up for the enemy's guided tour. Regardless of the many wrong stops available, God has a stop of destiny for each of us. A heavenly ticket has your name on it to make sure that you reach your divine destination. When you hear the boarding call, get on the train.

We'll make several stops in this book. I'll share what I went through at each stop. I trust my experience will prove that it's not worth getting off one stop early.

Until you have fasted and prayed, until you're walking on an elevated level with God, until you're positive that your spirit bears witness with the Conductor, I warn you, *don't get off the train!*

12

Chapter 1

Don't Get Off
the Train

The Lord told me that this life is like a train ride. We can't stop or get off until we have reached our destiny. Our life experiences are like a train ride with various routes or tracks that can be taken. Many attractions await us. Some may bring happiness; others are downright dangerous.

The Lord showed me in a vision that this train isn't typical. It has the ability to go anywhere because its route is orchestrated by the Holy Spirit. That means a person doesn't need to have a certain socioeconomic status for the train to stop for him or her.

God has designed this train to stop in the worst places. It runs on automatic, and God guides it to the gutter because He hears the cries of His people. The train heads to the divorce court because some passengers are down there. It will dash through Broken Heart Tunnel because some people need to be on the train.

Picking Up the Pitiful

Isn't it wonderful how God raises your lifestyle when He picks you up? God must transform the minds of these down-trodden passengers so that the Spirit of the Lord can pick them up body, soul, and spirit. God used King David to lift up such a lowly soul.

> And the king said, Is there not yet any of the house of Saul, that I may shew the kindness of God unto him? And Ziba said unto the king, Jonathan hath yet a son.... Then king David sent, and fetched him out of the house of Machir, the son of Ammiel, in Lodebar....And David said unto him, Fear not: for I will surely shew thee kindness for Jonathan thy father's sake, and will restore thee all the land of Saul thy father; and thou shalt eat bread at my table continually....So Mephibosheth dwelt in the Jerusalem: for he did eat continually at the king's table; and was lame on both his feet (2 Samuel 9:3,5,7,13).

This passage conveys awesome images in my mind. I imagine a train coming by, picking up Mephibosheth, and rescuing him from his resolve to be nothing.

Jonathan's crippled son lived in someone else's home. Even though he was the heir to better things, Mephibosheth was content to be pitiful and hopeless.

Have you ever quit hoping for something better? Did you feel the odds were stacked against you so high that you stopped praying for change? Perhaps you decided that God put you down there.

When God has a purpose for your life, He will send the train to pick you up and bring you into the presence of the King. The Lord sent a train to Lodebar, picked up this person who could not rescue himself, and put him in his rightful place. Sometimes the Lord has to rescue you from yourself.

When Suffering Safeguards You

The church does not want to deal with the issue of suffering. Did you know that painful situations in life often safeguard us from self-destructing? What do I mean? Look carefully at the latter portion of this chapter.

Mephibosheth had been rescued from despair and put in his rightful seat on the train. He ate continually from the master's table. This meant he had a relationship with the king. Living in the presence of the king, he also enjoyed royal blessings. One powerful phrase at the close of this passage, however, gives us a glimpse into God's infinite wisdom.

The Bible says that Mephibosheth was still lame in both his feet. That is powerful. Regardless of his newfound home and blessings, he still was not completely whole.

But I thought it was God's will for you to be healed. It is, but it's better to say God's will is for you not to perish. I'll say it like this: It's God's will that you not get off the train.

Some of you are bull-headed, though. If given the opportunity, you'll get out of your seat and walk off the train. You feel that you're strong enough to stand on your own two feet and step off the train.

Sometimes God has to handle you like Mephibosheth. You're lame when you stand on your own feet. If you don't have the Holy Spirit or the Conductor to stand by you, you'll fall right out the door. If Mephibosheth gets healed, he just may walk out of the palace. Because the Conductor knows this, He sometimes allows you to be buffeted. That helps you to realize you're not going to make it without some support.

We can't stop or get off the train until we've reached our divine destination. You're going through a difficult situation so that you'll learn how to stay in your appointed place.

My Own Journey

When I boarded the train, I was lame like Mephibosheth.

My marriage had failed, and I realized it had been a mistake from the beginning. I never should have gotten off the train, exchanging my relationship with God for a man. My ministry and finances began to dry up. I had no one to turn to. Who could understand what I was really feeling?

God used one of His "assistants" to get me on the train. Someone asked me to take care of a sick person in Detroit. Ironically, the person miraculously felt better when I arrived. She took me for a car ride into Port Huron. While we rode to church, the Spirit of the Lord spoke to this precious saint and told her to take me to New Hope Tabernacle. God had a divine appointment for me there.

I met Pastor and Sister William T. Nichols, who immediately invited me to minister that Sunday night in their church. The power of God moved greatly in that service. I saw a side of God that I had never experienced. There was a depth in God that I knew I didn't have.

Having been recently abandoned by my husband, I was like the lame man sitting at the master's table, eating the best spiritual food. The King had lavished His goodness upon me, yet I stood in the sanctuary lame.

I left with the memory of the presence of the King's palace in my mind and the experience of the King's power in my heart. Yet, I was still lame.

What drove me to the train?

I never forgot what it felt like being in the presence of God. I had experienced His royal touch. It was so awesome that I dreamed about it. Every waking moment, my heart panted for God's presence. Like the Song of Solomon says, "I sought him whom my soul loveth" (Song of Solomon 3:1). I had been struck by the blinding love of God's presence.

Love got me on the train!

I felt myself being persistently drawn by God. I knew the Conductor held a ticket with my name on it. Yes, I felt an overwhelming love for God, but I also recognized my obligation to the Conductor. I had to obey the instructions on the back of the ticket.

Because of many deaths, hazardous experiences, and tragic accidents, this ticket required one thing of me for the duration of the journey: Submit to the Conductor at all times. My reward? I would safely arrive at my destination.

At that point, I had to become totally dependent on God. I had to entrust my life to the man and woman of God whom I had just met. I embraced them as shepherds. I had to understand as a sheep, I was now too blind, too dumb, too inexperienced, and too young to see my way. I had to allow them to lead, guide, and show me the direction of God. I had to learn how to trust the voice of the Conductor, knowing that these assistants heard from God.

This train represents the power of God and His ability to lead you. It exemplifies His power to hold you up and strengthen you. You learn how to depend on God for your every need and for your every decision. If you understand this, you won't get off the train.

Your reserved seat has been designated by God. Each of us must stay in that seat until we have learned total surrender. We must learn to obey the voice of God. No one is exempt from this train ride–whether diseased, crippled, or mentally disturbed. They may be brokenhearted or spiritually bank-rupt, but there is still a seat for those who are willing to suf-fer the ride.

You may feel that you've already made it to your final des-tination, but this is the most detrimental stop. You've gotten off at "Hype".

Hype is a sensual stop; it appeals only to the emotions. It takes you for a ride until your senses have been tantalized, then dulled, and nothing else motivates you. Finally, you re-alize that you got off at the wrong stop. By the time you real-ize it, it might be too late. *Don't get off the train!*

Chapter 2

Wrong Time, Wrong Place

When you lose something valuable, even though it may be a sacrifice for the sake of the gospel, the pain could cause you to be shaken out of God. Some of you have already experienced this trauma, and you know what I'm talking about.

Simply put, our God is a jealous God. We've often put a negative connotation on jealousy, but each of us has a certain level of jealousy concerning things that are dear to us. Because God made us in His image, His creation takes on His character. When God renewed His covenant with Moses and the children of Israel, He issued a warning:

> Take heed to thyself, lest thou make a covenant with the inhabitants of the land whither thou goest, lest it be for a snare in the midst of thee:... For thou shalt worship no other god: for the Lord, whose name is Jealous, is a jealous God (Exodus 34:12,14).

Many of us ride the train of God's will until we come to the depot named Spouse. We're just fine as long as we're single and looking for the depot. We can follow the leading of the Spirit and do His will until the enemy sets a station on the route that catches our interest. Declaring that he or she is a part of God's plan, we stop the train to let a passenger on. The problem is, it's usually not time for the train to stop.

What if your spouse was the most precious thing to you and you lost him? I'm not talking about him being a little gift or a playtoy. I'm talking about the most precious thing in your life. That kind of loss produces a pain that you never forget. You can't eat. You can't sleep. You can't do anything but hurt.

Sometimes God asks us to make this ultimate sacrifice. He asks us to give up the very thing we thought we couldn't live without. God wants to know if you, like Abraham, are willing to slay Isaac to stay in His perfect will.

And he said, Take now thy son, thine *only* son Isaac, whom thou *lovest,* and get thee into the land of Moriah; and offer him there for a burnt offering upon one of the mountains which I will tell thee of (Genesis 22:2).

Can you imagine what Abraham felt when God spoke those words to him? Before he could take even one step toward Mt. Moriah, Abraham grieved the loss of his only son. What a price to pay–his only son. Before we deal with the pain and the price, let's look at the only son.

God Disregards Bad Tickets

The Lord made a profound statement to Abraham that many of us miss, but we need to heed. He told Abraham to take his *only* son. Before you overlook that, stop and think about that word *only.*

The Bible clearly states that Hagar, Sarah's bondwoman, had a son by Abraham named Ishmael. Ishmael was born before Isaac, and he was Abraham's son. Why did the Lord call Isaac, Abraham's only son? The answer goes to the heart of this book.

Abraham stopped the train by a bondwoman's tent and let someone on for a ride. When the Holy Spirit, the Conductor, came by asking for tickets, Hagar, the bondwoman, didn't have a ticket stamped in Heaven. Even though she rode long enough to become pregnant, she wasn't pregnant with the promise from Heaven.

Many times in our lives we stop the train by some foreign tent and pick up passengers who we think are in the will of God. These passengers produce seed, but they don't produce promised seed.

When the Lord said *only* to Abraham, He disregarded the pitstop that Abraham had made on his own accord. This did not mean that He would not bless him, because He promised to bless Abraham's seed. It meant that Isaac was the seed of promise and therefore Abraham's only son.

And God said unto Abraham, Let it not be grievous in thy sight because of the lad, and because of thy bondwoman; in all that Sarah hath said unto thee, hearken unto her voice; for in Isaac shall thy seed be called. And also of the son of the bondwoman will I make a nation, because he is thy seed (Genesis 21:12,13).

A promised seed has a ticket that has been stamped in Heaven. When the Lord asks for the ticket and He doesn't see His personal stamp, He disregards the bogus ticket. He doesn't even acknowledge that the mess is there. He just stops the train and tells Abraham to inform Hagar and Ishmael that they have to get off.

And Abraham rose up early in the morning, and took bread, and a bottle of water, and gave it unto Hagar, putting it on her shoulder, and the child, and sent her away: and she departed, and wandered in the wilderness of Beersheba (Genesis 21:14).

Now that must have been really painful to Abraham, but that was not the ultimate pain. You have to be willing to feel the ultimate pain in order to experience the ultimate gain! You must know this one fact: There are no free tickets on this train.

Trapped on the Train

The apostle Paul said that he was a prisoner. He was tied to his seat on the train. Like Paul, we need to become voluntarily trapped on the train.

> I therefore, the prisoner of the Lord, beseech you that ye walk worthy of the vocation wherewith ye are called (Ephesians 4:1).

Here's where a lot of Christians miss it. We don't want to become prisoners, yet we want to call Him Lord. You can't call Him Lord if you're not His prisoner. You must decide to be trapped. You must decide to be enclosed. When you're willing to be bound, you are willing to be governed.

I don't care what I have to go through. I won't let go of Jesus. I don't care how much trouble it causes. I don't care whom I have to lose on the way. I'm not going to let go of Jesus.

When you come to this point, then you can truly call Him Lord. Why? Because He not only masters you, He also governs you. He declares your boundaries. He also confirms His great love to you, even in the midst of difficulty.

> Who shall separate us from the love of Christ? shall tribulation, or distress, or persecution, or famine, or nakedness, or peril, or sword? As it is written, For thy sake we are killed all the day long; we are accounted as sheep for the slaughter. Nay, in all these things we are more than conquerors through him that loved us. For I am persuaded, that neither death,

nor life, nor angels, nor principalities, nor powers, nor things present, nor things to come, nor height, nor depth, nor any other creature, shall be able to separate us from the love of God, which is in Christ Jesus our Lord (Romans 8:35-39).

What was Paul saying? He declared, "I have my seat on the train. I have my ticket. Not everyone will be happy with my decision. I may have to endure a lot. I may have to go without. None of this will surprise me because I read the boarding rules. I am oblivious to outside distractions.

"This might even cost me my life. Because I boarded of my own free will, I might as well stay on for the long haul. Regardless of whom I might lose or who might not like me, I will not give up my seat nor get off this train. I have been commanded by the Conductor to stay on this train until I reach my destination."

A Difficult Journey

You might say, "You have no idea how hard it is!"

I do. I can totally empathize with those who struggle with the demands Christ puts on our lives.

Do you know how I started out? I delivered my first message at age ten. I was in a small church, and they asked me to be a junior speaker. My message was on the four sections of the heart. After that I began to read poems and different things. I began to minister at a young age.

When I was around 17, I began preaching in many churches of various sizes. Thinking back, the essence of this book became a reality in my life at this point.

On many occasions, I had ridden the train to different locations. In retrospect, I remember arriving at my place of destination. I rode the train one day into a small city called Port

Huron, Michigan. As I got off the train, I met a woman and her husband, Pastor William T. Nichols. I embraced this man and woman of God.

Immediately, the Lord began to show this woman of God things about me and about my life that I had never shared with anyone–emotional traumas and difficulties. She began to speak to me about divine appointment. These people began to see things about my future that a lot of people are not ordained to see unless it is a part of God's will.

I didn't understand how far the train was going to go, but I got off at that stop. I remained in that particular destination for nine years. The Lord broke me in this place. One of His faithful servants initiated this deep work in me. This man of God boldly spoke some things that changed my life forever.

Pastor Nichols said, "You're gifted and talented, but when the ministry and the church get through using you, they'll take the next fresh piece of meat that comes along."

It was shocking, but he continued.

"I want you to learn, but not just surface things. You need to learn the anointing. You need to learn purpose. You need to learn who you are. I want you to stay in Port Huron for awhile."

The next thing he said really shook me.

"Hand me your black book with all your appointments. Cancel all of your engagements and tell people that you don't preach anymore."

Imagine what went through my mind. That was really traumatic.

One thing that I really love about the Lord is that He will not leave you in limbo without giving you purpose.

Your Divine Destiny

Pastor Nichols told me that God would raise me up one day. He said no one would ever be able to stop my anointing. He said I had to go through the process of allowing the facade to come off. All the ugliness about Juanita Bynum had to surface. By doing this, God could create in me what He wanted me to be. God would prepare me to be a world changer.

I had learned to be an evangelist. Until that point, no one had taught me how to get anointed. As unpopular as this statement is, I must say it. Books, tapes, and prayer don't anoint you. The anointing comes only through the fire.

I am not seeking to win a popularity contest, but I do want to take people to the next level in God. If you stick with me through this book, you will be able to recognize when you come to the stop called divine destination.

How? You will feel a pain that will cry out from your soul. Discontentment will be in the very fiber of your being. Restlessness will be in your heart. Your vision will become blurred. Your speech will be stammered. Your hearing will be dim. Yet, in the midst of all of that, you know within your spirit that you're in the right place. You will know that you're at the right station and content to stay there until . . .

Not until I am recognized. *Not* until someone calls my name. *Not* until I get a title. No, none of that moves me anymore. I'm going to stay here until God gives me clear vision. My hearing is keen. My speech is compared with no one. My heart is transformed, and my mind is renewed. I'm ready at that point, not to get back on the train, but to lead others to depots where their train awaits to pick them up.

Cut Away the Flesh

Heaven convened a board meeting concerning you. Sometimes you have to cut back in certain areas to increase your profit. Productivity may suffer in the short-term, but you can expect long-term profit when the process is over. The Lord may have to circumcise your flesh, but it's to protect and ensure your productivity while rolling away the stains of the past.

Before the children of Israel reached their destiny, they had to endure a painful procedure. The Lord instructed Joshua to cut away their flesh before they entered the Promised Land.

At that time the Lord said unto Joshua, Make thee sharp knives, and circumcise again the children of Israel the second time. And Joshua made him sharp knives and circumcise again the children of Israel at the hill of the foreskins. And this is the cause why Joshua did circumcise: All the people that came out of Egypt, that were males, even all the men of war, died in the wilderness by the way, after they came out of Egypt....And the Lord said unto Joshua, This day have I rolled away the reproach of Egypt from off you (Joshua 5:2-4;9a).

Some things can't be a part of your destiny. Sometimes the Lord has to cut you again and again. These Israelites had been born in the wilderness. They were born during tough times. They did not have the luxuries of life. God will allow you to go through the hard times so that you can be prepared for your destiny. If you know you've been called and chosen, get ready. The flesh is about to be cut away, and it will hurt.

I Stepped Off the Train

I remember feeling like I had something to prove to myself and others. I was a churchgoer, but I can't honestly say that I was connected to leadership. I was not connected in the spirit enough for the voice of leadership to govern my decisions.

I remember coming out of a relationship that was actually a self-imagined relationship. What do I mean by that? I was more in love with someone than he was with me.

After learning that the person really did not have the kind of feelings for me that I desired, I moved on and met my future husband. The timing was perfect. He said everything that I wanted to hear. He was ministering to me, not in terms of the Lord, yet meeting a felt need in me.

Actually, I was like the man at the gate called Beautiful. The disciples told him "Silver and gold have I none; but such as I have give I thee" (Acts 3:6). Like the lame man, I had another need. What I thought I needed was not what I really needed.

As time went on, one thing led to another. An imaginary wedding began to play in my mind, which I believe causes a lot of people to step out of God's will to marry the wrong partner. That's why Scripture says we are to "[cast] down imaginations, and every high thing that exalteth itself against the knowledge of God" (2 Cor. 10:5).

What is hindering the purpose of God in your life? I began to ask myself that question. God gave me some checks in my spirit, but I ignored them.

While looking in the windows of jewelry stores after work, I caught the sparkle of wedding rings. Besides giving me a one-carat diamond ring, my husband-to-be was very attractive. I was drawn by his good looks. Unfortunately, I didn't know that marriage involved a lot more than sex.

Marriage is ministry. That means not only receiving ministry, but being mature enough to return ministry back to the other party. Both partners need to be committed to Christ, then to each other, and filled with the Holy Ghost to build a successful marriage.

I used to say that my marriage failed because of me. I based that on the apostle Paul's words that the husband "is sanctified by the wife" (1 Cor. 7:14). I didn't consider that "every wise woman buildeth her house" (Proverbs 14:1).

Listen carefully. The woman builds the house. Even though I kept a clean house and did everything I knew to do, I hadn't accumulated enough power in my walk with God to save the marriage.

A sanctified wife has gone through a period of purification before marriage. Had I purified my life, enabling me to live intimately with the Holy Spirit? Did I have the discernment to know what forces were trying to destroy my marriage? I wish I knew then what I know now about the spiritual realm. Wives need discernment and power in prayer to go after those enemies.

God is a jealous God, and I grieved Him in this relationship. The man became "it". There was no more praying. There was no more fasting. There was no more reverencing God. I had a one-track mind. I just wanted to walk down the aisle. I wanted to wear a wedding dress. I wanted to have a sit-down dinner. I wanted to take pictures in front of the Buckingham fountain. I wanted to be glamorous. I wanted my day, not knowing that it was the wrong stop.

Even though I was self-willed in pursuing the relationship, and it eventually disintegrated, God used the event to break me. I grew to want only His will in all my relationships.

Marriage is the right stop for many of us, but we have to stop in the right season.

> In every thing by prayer and supplication with thanksgiving let your requests be made known unto God. And the peace of God, which passeth all understanding, shall keep your hearts and minds through Christ Jesus (Philippians 4:6,7).

That means that if you don't get your spouse through prayer and supplication, you have him illegally and the marriage will not last. Anything not received through prayer and supplication has been obtained illegally; therefore it doesn't have strength to remain. At some point in life, sooner or later, you'll lose it. Before you make the next big decision, check your arrival time and place and make sure your tickets match. Until that time comes, rest content and be kept by the Lord.

Purpose in Pain

The apostle Paul told Timothy that God had a purpose in all the heartaches and sufferings. It doesn't always feel good, but there's reason for the pain.

> For the which cause I also suffer these things: nevertheless I am not ashamed: for I know whom I have believed, and am persuaded that he is able to keep that which I have committed unto him against that day (2 Timothy 1:12).

What am I saying? Many times God allows us to go through some things so we can recognize that we need Him. If you never had a problem, you would never need a solution. The more you need Him, the more you call on Him. The more you call on Him, the more He shows up. The more He shows up, the better you know Him. That's the ultimate reason: that you might know Him.

I know Jesus Christ as a Provider. I know Him as a Protector. I know Him as a Friend. I know Him as a Keeper. He kept me! He kept me when I couldn't keep myself. He kept me when I was messed up in my mind.

Thou wilt keep him in perfect peace, whose mind is stayed on thee: because he trusteth in thee (Isaiah 26:3).

Chapter 3

Trivial Pursuit

Jesus spoke powerful words to His disciples. The Lord always prepared His disciples for what was to come. We often forget that He does the same thing for us. Look at the following passage:

> No man can serve two masters: for either he will hate the one, and love the other; or else he will hold to the one, and despise the other. Ye cannot serve God and mammon. Therefore I say unto you, Take no thought for your life, what ye shall eat, or what ye shall drink; nor yet for your body, what ye shall put on. Is not the life more than meat, and the body than raiment? (Matthew 6:24,25).

Jesus spoke truth that applied to more than those early disciples. God's Word is the same yesterday, today, and forever. I believe the Lord was speaking prophetically concerning the present day church.

We live in a time where the primary focus of every Christian is tomorrow. We worry about what we are going to eat tomorrow. What am I going to wear tomorrow? Where am I going tomorrow? We get so caught up in temporal things that we make decisions based solely on that. We totally take God out of the picture. We don't depend on Him. We always plan for a rainy day. Everybody is concerned about "me"!

We preach about money to keep living. We prophesy about houses and cars. We have financial conferences. We have banquets and fundraisers to make sure that Ms. Jones' lights don't get turned off. All of this consumes us when Jesus specifically said, "Take no thought."

Look at the words of the Lord. "Is not the life more than meat . . .?" What was He saying? Don't you care more about souls than making sure there's food in your refrigerator? Many of us are so busy working for ourselves that we can't work for God. I believe the Holy Spirit is grieved when we sweat more out of church than we do in church. We concentrate more on the job than we do on the Word. We meditate more on the melody than on the lyrics.

What am I trying to say? Many of us stop the train and get off so that we can obtain things–we do this in the name of eternal life.

A House of Prostitutes?

Many of us are just like the rich young ruler. We come to God for eternal life. "Master, what must I do to inherit something? If I come to church, can I have a blessing? If I get on the usher board, can I have a blessing? If I attend Sunday school, will You bless me? Master, I listen to the sermon on Sunday. I read my Bible. I don't curse. I don't lie. I think I deserve something for that. Master, Master, send down Your blessing."

Herein lies one of the major flaws in the church today. Everyone wants to prostitute God.

I know I'm about to get in trouble now. How can I use that term in relation to God? Well, let's look at it this way. A prostitute gives something in return for receiving something. She yields her body for payment. Isn't that what many of us want God to do?

"God, I will come to church if You bless me. God, I will pay tithes if You bless me. God, I will sing in the choir if You bless me. I will give You something in return for Your goods. I will give You if You give me."

You tell me what that sounds like.

What if God doesn't bless you? What if He doesn't show up when you think He should? God wants to know, "Are you willing to give up everything to have Me? Are you willing to go without to have Me?"

That's commitment. It's not a give-and-take relationship; it's unconditional. I know that's hard, but it's the truth. That's why not everyone can be a disciple. Not everyone has discipline. We must be willing to give up everything.

Leaving Our First Love

Many of us stop interceding for others and start praying for cars. We stop fasting to submit our flesh to God, and now we fast for a house. We stop going to prayer services, and now we go to fundraisers. We stop worshiping God in the beauty of holiness, and now we wave at God in the beauty of Donna Karen and Armani suits. We don't go to church to see a move of God; we go to church to see the new fashions.

Jesus spoke profoundly to the church at Ephesus about this.

I know thy works, and thy labour, and thy patience, and how thou canst not bear them which are evil: and thou has tried them which say they are apostles, and are not, and hast found

33

them liars: And hast borne, and hast patience, and for my name's sake hast laboured, and hast not fainted. Nevertheless, I have somewhat against thee, because thou hast left thy first love. Remember therefore from whence thou art fallen, and repent, and do the first works; or else I will come unto thee quickly, and will remove thy candlestick out of his place, except thou repent (Revelation 2:2-5).

The Lord said that you started off fine. You did what you were asked to do. You came to church faithfully. You were in every prayer meeting. You lived a fasted life. You stayed in the Word. You were not easily deceived, but something happened. For some reason you stopped the train. The enemy offered you some bait, and you took it. You put on the brakes.

And the Lord said, "I have something against you. I'm not well pleased with you because you left your first love. You were sitting on the train doing just fine, but you looked out the window. You saw something that looked good to you, but it wasn't good for you. I told you that I would bless and care for you, but something grabbed your attention."

Diverted from Destiny

How can you tell when your attention is divided? You can't complete one thing because your mind is somewhere else. Let me tell you this. You can let something divert your attention, but it will cost you your place in God. Ask Adam and Eve. One blink of the eye can cost you everything.

And when the woman saw that the tree was good for food, and that it was pleasant to the eyes, and a tree to be desired to make one wise, she took of the fruit thereof, and did eat, and gave also unto her husband with her; and he did eat (Genesis 3:6).

What happened to the woman when she stopped the train? Allow me to paraphrase. The woman was sitting on the train just enjoying herself. She had been in constant communion with God. She had heard the voice of God, but she started listening to someone else. Be careful of talking to the other passengers. One of them might be a snake.

When Eve took her eyes off God, the enemy immediately attracted her to something else. She saw the fruit on one forbidden tree. She wasn't really hungry because she had just eaten from the Master's table. A lingering look told her that the tree was good for food. She had not even tasted it; she only gazed upon it. One look at the fruit divided her attention. In essence, she left her first love.

Other things can quickly become the object of your desire. If the enemy can get you to take your eyes off God, he can change your desires. Don't get me wrong. God will give you the desires of your heart, but that is contingent on the orientation of your heart.

> Trust in the Lord, and do good; so shalt thou dwelt in the land, and verily thou shalt be fed. Delight thyself also in the Lord; and he shall give thee the desires of thine heart (Psalm 37:3,4).

When your heart is in the right place, your desires will be in the right place. Eve was more concerned about being God than enjoying the fruits of being the apple of God's eye. Because her heart was in the wrong place, her desire left God and went in the direction of a piece of fruit. Think about that. Giving up everything to get a piece of fruit.

God recognizes where your heart is by what comes out of your mouth. Remember, out of the abundance of the heart the mouth speaks. Eve said that they could not touch nor eat of the tree of knowledge.

That statement wasn't true. God never said anything about not touching the tree. The enemy had an avenue to attack. For a moment she braked the train and forgot about her fellowship with God. She forgot how He comforted her. She forgot how He provided. She stopped delighting in the Lord. If you delight in Him, your desires will be in the right place and He will meet them.

I remember when I stopped my train. I saw somebody cute and got off the train. God had other plans for me, but I went for what I saw. Many times we get off track and God has to bring us back. We will never reach our true destination if God allows us to stay on that track. God has a preset time for you to arrive at this place. He often moves people who will slow down the train.

Listen to me carefully. If it's not God's will, it will never work. It may take you 15 years to realize it, but it isn't going to work! You may be married 21 years, but it will never work. If it isn't God, it will never work.

Why? Because anyone who gets on your train–if he or she isn't supposed to be there–will have to be removed. They may ride for a couple of blocks, a year, or maybe even a few years. Eventually, however, God will say, "All right, Joe. Enough of this mess. Get off!"

Chapter 4

For Such a Time as This

When God has a work for you to do, He has His way of bringing it to pass. Sometimes you don't understand His method, but the results are crystal clear.

Well, at least that's the case in my life. You see, I can't talk about anyone like I can myself. I can hear some of you saying, "Well, Sister Bynum, I'm married to this man or I'm married to this woman..."

Let me interrupt you right there. You're just like me—you got off the train. Many people make mistakes but don't admit them. I believe in telling the truth. I believe in helping people avoid some of the mistakes I made. Some of us forget where we came from. We act like we've never done anything wrong. Stop lying! I love the way Jesus exposes us for who we really are.

And the scribes and Pharisees brought unto him a woman taken in adultery; and when they had set her in the midst, they say unto him, Master, this woman was taken in adultery, in the very act. Now Moses in the law commanded us, that such should be stoned: but what sayest thou?...

So when they continued asking him, he lifted up himself, and said unto them, He that is without sin among you, let him first cast a stone at her. And again he stooped down, and wrote on the ground. And they which heard it, being convicted by their own conscience, went out one by one, beginning at the eldest, even unto the last: and Jesus was left alone, and the woman standing in the midst (John 8:3-5,7-9).

Jesus told those Pharisees that they may wear clean suits and boast of big titles, but beneath that they hide secret sins. They were no different than this woman. Isn't it funny how we can be so holy when our sin isn't exposed? If everyone knew everything about you, you would never leave your house. Many of us have pulled the train into a dark depot where we have done some dirty things.

I thank God for the conviction that He put in me. It didn't come easy. I paid a price to assist in your deliverance. Believe it or not, I went through some things to help you. You can't minister effectively in an area that you haven't been through.

Can you imagine the ministry this woman had after this incident? Her sin was not just heard about; she was caught in the very act. There was absolutely no denying it. Have you noticed something about a person who has been through hell and everyone knows it? He or she has nothing to lose.

This woman could go from place to place and tell people about the forgiving power of Jesus. She could tell how He can use an outcast. She could witness of His infinite mercy. I praise God for showing me imperfect people who found favor in the sight of God.

Don't Be Deceived!

I remember when I stopped my train–knowing that God had other plans for me. At the time, however, I went for what

I saw. You may be in a similar predicament. Don't get off the train!

That man may have already told you that he loved you. He has been saying all the right things. You say to yourself, "This must be God. No one can tell me that it isn't. The devil is a liar. This is the one. I've heard from God."

Isn't it funny how we hear from God when it's convenient? Any other time, we buy tapes and books to learn how to hear from God. Yes, I know. He likes you. He's going to do this, and he's going to do that. He has promised you the world. All of that is fine, but is he in the will of God for your life? If so, is it the right time?

This is the hard part–letting people go who are in the way. To you, he or she is not in the way. You feel that this person will enhance your ministry. You believe he will take care of that part of your life. Wrong!

God says, "If you let him stay, you're going to get off track." Your attention will be divided. You won't pray enough. You'll never want to fast. When he's talking, you can't hear from God.

The timing is all wrong. I can see the train slowing down. When things get to that point, God will remove the hindrance. You may weep, but he's got to go. You may whine, but she can't stay. I know you're going to pout for a while, but it's for your own good. If the Lord doesn't remove this obstacle, you're going to trip over it.

Johnny doesn't have a ticket; he has to go. Susie may be a fine woman, but she doesn't have a ticket. She needs to leave now. Ricky's train departs at a later hour. Sorry, maybe later.

Every hindrance must be removed. This train is destined for glory, and only passengers who can contribute can be a part of this crew. God is bringing you out of the shadows and into the kingdom for such a time as this. All aboard!

Chapter 5

When the Time is Right

So many people chomp at the bit, wanting to know when God will use them. Most don't have enough patience to wait on God. You may feel that you're ready now.

God wants me to tell you to wait until He says you're ready. If you don't wait, you're going to blow it and derail your train.

Remember Peter, the bold and boisterous disciple? He didn't wait for the action to come to him. He usually acted first and repented later. In his zeal, Peter rebuked Jesus when He started talking about how He had to die.

Many of you are just like Peter. You feel like you know what's right, and you need to make the decisions for both you and the Lord. I'm so glad that the Lord looked beyond my stupidity and saw my vulnerability.

I'm glad that I serve a God Who knows what's going to happen before it happens. He recognizes our shortcomings long before we ever do. You may have thought that your mistakes surprised God, but He doesn't need the 911 system.

God doesn't get alarmed when something goes wrong. He knows the end from the beginning. God allows you to mess up so that you can see where *you* are.

Sifted Like Wheat

As Jesus told the disciples about the kingdom they were appointed to rule over, they swelled up with pride. Their eyes got big, and they began to walk with a swagger. Think how you responded when someone prophesied how great you're going to be. They told you how large your ministry will be. They commented on how anointed you are.

As Jesus revealed this, He could see Peter perk up. His zeal began to show. He was kicking his heels, ready to take on the world. Jesus may have said to Himself, "I had better burst this balloon. I better let him know that the enemy is listening to this too, and he's not going to make it easy on him."

Let's look at the exact words of Jesus:

And I appoint unto you a kingdom, as my Father hath appointed unto me; that ye may eat and drink at my table in my kingdom, and sit on thrones judging the twelve tribes of Israel. And the Lord said, Simon, Simon, behold, Satan hath desired to have you, that he may sift you as wheat: But I have prayed for thee, that thy faith fail not: and when thou art converted, strengthen thy brethren (Luke 22:29-32).

Let me make this very clear. The devil hates you, and he never takes a break. Jesus told Simon, "Satan hath desired to have you." I want to get that message out to the body of Christ. Satan desires to have you.

This has an interesting connotation. The devil wants to get intimate with you. He wants to take advantage of you. He wants to lure you into a position of compromise.

Jesus said, "I know you think you're ready, but the enemy isn't going to roll over and die. He's going to watch you and follow you until just the right moment. When you drop your guard, he's going to manipulate your every move."

Jesus said that Satan would sift you as wheat. You must understand that this is a process. Many of you underestimate the enemy. Just because you survived one temptation, that doesn't mean that the devil is through.

Your enemy is cunning. He will slowly eat away at you. He will get you to stop being faithful in church. He will cut your prayer time in half by offering something to do instead. It may be a new club. It may be a new job. The enemy will use what you thought was a blessing and make it a hindrance.

He desires to sift you. It's almost like an hour glass. As the sand begins to fall through, you don't really notice it until a significant amount has fallen. What do I mean? You may still be able to preach. You might still feel that you are anointed. You may even be pastoring a church, but slowly the sand is falling. Time is running out. You've taken on too much, and you don't even know it. Soon you're caught in a downward spiral with nothing to hold on to. Every aspect of your life is headed down hill. You're doing things you never thought you would do. Satan has sifted you to nothing. What will you do when the fiery darts hit? Will you get off the train?

Thank God, Jesus did not stop with Satan's desire to have and sift you. Thank God, Someone is watching your back. Jesus has already prayed for you that your faith will not fail. You know that prayer has been answered. Thank You, Jesus.

If You Think You're Ready . . .

Jesus didn't say you wouldn't take a hard hit. He didn't say you wouldn't fall. I want to talk to those who have taken a few hard hits. You may have even taken a dangerous fall. I know you don't want to talk about it, but it's the truth. Peter took a pretty good hit, but not without warning.

> And he said unto him, Lord, I am ready to go with thee, both into prison, and to death. And he said, I tell thee, Peter, the cock shall not crow this day, before that thou shalt thrice deny that thou knowest me (Luke 22:33,34).

The Lord told Peter, "You're not where you think you are. If I leave you to yourself, you're going to blow it. You're open prey for the enemy right now, but you think you're covered with armor."

This is what happens to many ministers. You think you're ready. You've learned a few Scriptures. Someone told you that you can preach, and now you want to ask God the ultimate question: What's taking You so long?

God says to the zealous person, "There's a depot marked Ministry, but it's not your time yet." You need to go back to the fields until you are ready to handle the giant. I know you think that you are anointed–and you very well may be–but your anointing may not be for this season. Remember David was anointed to be king over Israel, but he was not ready to reign yet.

David was anointed as a youth, but that wasn't his time to take the throne. He had a season, but he had to wait for it. He was willing to return to the fields and work until his time came.

Many of you don't want to go through this part of your ministry. Are you willing to be anointed and remain faithful until it is your time? You need to pass several tests to prepare you for the giant. David fought a lion and a bear before he confronted Goliath. Are you willing to learn from preparatory tests before you take the final exam? Like David, you'll be ready to defeat the giant, which will catapult you into the spotlight.

> And David said unto Saul, Thy servant kept his father's sheep, and there came a lion, and a bear, and took a lamb out of the flock: And I went out after him, and smote him, and delivered it out of his mouth: and when he arose against me, I caught him by his beard, and smote him, and slew him. Thy servant slew both the lion and the bear: and this uncircumcised Philistine shall be as one of them, seeing he hath defied the armies of the living God. David said moreover, The Lord that delivered me out of the paw of the lion, and out of the paw of the bear, he will deliver me out of the hand of this Philistine. And Saul said unto David, Go, and the Lord be with thee (1 Samuel 17:34-37).

There's a price for the position. When you can pay the price, you can have the position. When the Conductor comes through, you may have a whole congregation on your train. You might even be preaching.

If it's not your time, He will say, "Hold it! What's going on here? Ticket! Ticket! Revival over! You have to get off the train. It's not time for you to preach! It's not time for you to cast out demons and lay hands on the sick! It's not time for you to come into your ministry yet! You're not at the depot called Ministry!"

Bursting My Bubble

God greatly used me during my time at Port Huron, and many young people were excited about my ministry. The way the Lord used me in that meeting was awesome. That was truly a phenomenal move of God. My bubble was about to burst, however.

. The man of God mentioned to me about staying on in the city. I immediately had to deal with my motives. Many people, especially those who are cloaked with a garment of great ministry, are often enticed to use the ministry for gain before their purification.

I was deceived by the way the Lord used me; therefore, I became convinced that it was my time. The man of God told me that I wasn't ready.

I thought to myself, "What do you mean, I'm not ready? Do you see how people fall out? Do you hear the testimonies of what God has done through me?"

People were healed in my meeting. Sinners got saved in that meeting that others had prayed for for years. What did he mean I wasn't ready?

At this point I was awakened to the difference between the power of the ministry and the spirit of the person. I had to be willing to give up the mantle and the cloak of the power so that I could really see the person.

When the real person came alive, I was in a place where the people who had seen me in my glory had to see me in my worst state. They had to see my bad attitude. They had to watch me be rebuked. They had to watch me go through a failing marriage and endure the gossip and scorn.

Those same people who saw me in suede shoes, the beautiful dresses, and gorgeous hairstyles now passed my apartment in the projects. They saw me living with no furniture except a donated kitchen table. They saw me working at McDonald's at night and Sears during the day. I also did hair on the weekends just to make ends meet. When I became feeble, they saw me. They watched me in the welfare lines to get money and food stamps and cheese. I cried out many days, "Where are You, God?" What happened to all those prophecies?

The only thing I had was a ticket. When I didn't know anything else, I knew I had a ticket. I knew I had a place in the kingdom of God for ministry. I knew that at a certain time, God was going to raise me up. The time of waiting to be transformed is the killer.

Yes, I had spurts where I would lead worship and the church would be shaken to the foundation. Even after being there five or six years, my pastor's wife would say, "No, that ain't it." Every time that I had done something that I thought would give me some notoriety and prove that I was all right, they would still tell me that I was not at the level nor power to get to my final destination.

You've got to be connected to someone who knows the realm and the power that is necessary to fulfill the mandate. There are a lot of anointings–tangible anointings–but I'm talking about a level in God that is beyond flesh.

My Time of Tarrying

How do you think I felt searching for something that I had never experienced before? I can imagine what the disciples must have felt as they waited in the upper room. They had no idea what Pentecost would be like. Like my predecessors, I waited for something that I didn't recognize. No one could tell me how it felt. I would just know it when it came. Like the disciples, I had a ticket, which actually was a word from God: "Go and wait until it comes!"

I had to go and tarry, an old church term used years ago. I'm not talking about "tarrying" like the theologians described it as just waiting. I'm talking about the tarrying of the old school, where your voice is gone and your sides ache. When you finish this kind of tarrying, there are no more tears. All I could do was moan, but still that was not the level. You have spurts of the glory of God hit the flesh, but still that's not it.

During this time, I had another rude awakening. After seven years of tarrying, I discovered I had been doing it for the wrong reason. I was tarrying to regain the popularity that I once had. I wanted to be recognized again. I wanted my place back.

So, how do you know when you've got it back?

You know that you have reached that level when a particular place is not important. You know when you're not moved by what people say about you anymore. Whether it's praise or persecution, it just doesn't matter. You know when you're not upset because someone else is sitting in your usual seat.

You have reached the level then, because you finally realize that you have a ticket in your spirit. You know that you have been validated through the Spirit and not through the person. You have actually reached that level when everyone else is saying that you're nothing, and it doesn't hinder you because you know who you are in God.

Who you are in God will always contradict who men say that you are. That's why the Bible says, "Woe unto you, when all men shall speak well of you" (Luke 6:26). If you start pleasing man, there must be something about you that is not pleasing to the Father.

Therefore, in the process of searching for the place that God wanted me to be in, I had to tarry. I had to wait. I had to suffer humiliation. I had to hear, "She'll never be anything." I had to become dismantled from everything that I knew to be familiar. When everything around you is foreign, that is when the Potter is starting to put you together.

You don't recognize your shout anymore. You fall to the floor and the presence of the Lord hits you and produces a new dance. Your praise doesn't sound the same. The tears on your face are no longer water but liquid fire. Your hands quiver. You do things that you don't recognize. That's when you know that you're tapping an unfamiliar level in God. That's when the old Juanita died and true ministry came alive.

What is true ministry?

True ministry is a burden for anyone. Race doesn't matter. Creed doesn't matter. Color doesn't matter. The person can be fat, skinny, tall, or short. That's the burden of the Lord that Ezekiel talked about. Your heart goes where God's heart goes. You and God weep over the same things. You're sensitive to what touches Him. You care for the same things. That's when you know that you've just gotten off at the stop of "true ministry."

When you're still looking for a title, prestige, or a name, you're not at the level. If a name becomes your search or pursuit, then you're looking to be marketed and not to be poured out in true ministry.

In my search to know whether I was ready for true ministry, these were the signs. When they ask you to preach, you won't think you're ready. When they ask you to lead worship, you won't have a song in your heart. When you get up with no agenda, however, and the people of God are blessed, that's when you know you have tapped into "true ministry." You know that you've gotten off at the right stop.

Chapter 6

Everyone Can't Ride

Along the tracks, there are many depots. You're not supposed to stop at every depot, however. Some depots are appropriate places to stop and refuel. Not everyone at that station will be able to board the train. Many people may want to get on, but if they're going to hinder what God is doing in your life, then you must prohibit them from boarding.

You may even have to put some people off the train who have been riding with you. Why? They may have completed God's purpose at this time in your life.

> To every thing there is a season, and a time to every purpose under the heaven: A time to be born, and a time to die; a time to plant, and a time to pluck up that which is planted (Ecclesiastes 3:1,2).

Solomon, the wisest man who ever lived, encouraged us to respect the seasons of our lives. This ruffles some feathers because we don't want to release our grasp on certain things—or people. No matter how difficult it gets, we still want to hang on to the familiar.

Let me tell you something. If you're too full, there's no room to add anything. Sometimes people who hang on to you need to be released so God can bring about the next move in your life.

Everyone is not meant to like you. You will not be the apple of everyone's eye. You will not be able to please everyone. Stop trying! Everybody is *not* a part of the purpose that God has for your life.

A Help or Hindrance?

After people have served God's purpose for a certain season in your life, it's OK to release them to their next assignment. Solomon said there's a time to plant, and a time to pluck up that which is planted. What does that mean? Some people will have to be dismissed from your train.

They may beg you, but they have to go. They may kick and scream, but they have to go. They may even cry, but you have to terminate their tenure. Your ultimate purpose is to fulfill His purpose. If they can't help you with your purpose, then they will hinder your purpose.

Certain men would help Gideon fulfill his call to deliver Israel from the Midianites. Others, however, would hinder him. God tested and separated these men until He had exactly what Gideon needed to rout the enemy.

And the Lord said unto Gideon, The people that are with thee are too many for me to give the Midianites into their hands, lest Israel vaunt themselves against me, saying, Mine own hand hath saved me. Now therefore go to, proclaim in the ears of the people, saying, Whosoever is fearful and afraid, let him return and depart early from mount Gilead. And their returned of the people twenty and two thousand; and there remained ten thousand (Judges 7:2,3).

The Lord said to Gideon, "You have too many people in your entourage to fulfill My purpose. I can never make you into what I intended if you don't thin out the crowd around you."

I'm sure that Gideon had some friends in the bunch, but they were not a part of God's blueprints for this time in Gideon's life. If they aren't designed for this season, they have to go.

Sometimes your so-called friends won't have the right motives. They just want to get as much from you as they can. These people are leeches. They serve no purpose but to take from you. God will grant you a peaceful parting with them—if you heed His first warning.

Gideon gave them a reason to leave. He told them if you fear where God is about to take us, then leave and there will be no hard feelings.

Those who left represent people who had served their purpose. They were once comfortable and comforting to you, but now they get on your nerves and seem to get in the way. Most of the time, these people won't hurt too much by leaving. You can bid them a fond farewell and go on with your life.

Many of you need to do this right now. God has told you to end a certain relationship, but you're afraid to obey Him. Go ahead. God will make it easy for you. It won't be hard. Go ahead. You need to get rid of the easy ones because the hard job is coming. Look at what happened to Gideon.

And the Lord said unto Gideon, The people are yet too many; bring them down unto the water, and I will try them for thee there: and it shall be, that of whom I say unto thee, This shall go with thee, the same shall go with thee; and of whomsoever I say unto thee, This shall not go with thee, the same shall not go (Judges 7:4).

There are people whom you will never put off the train unless the Lord tells you to. These are your bosom buddies, your good friends. If they hinder God's purpose for your life, however, they become snakes in the grass. You may not recognize them until you've been bitten. That's why God told you to get rid of them.

They may almost destroy you before you recognize them. They could very well be on your staff. They may come to every prayer meeting. They may be a part of your worship team. They may even be your armor bearer. But if they're not in the plan, they must go.

The Lord told Gideon that He would try his staff. He would put them in a position to show their true colors. In this place of separation, the spotlight will provide answers to the ultimate question: Will they fight with you or help the enemy to defeat you?

So he brought down the people unto the water: and the Lord said unto Gideon, Every one that lappeth of the water with his tongue, as a dog lappeth, him shalt thou set by himself; likewise every one that boweth down upon his knees to drink. And the number of them that lapped, putting their hand to their mouth, were three hundred men: but all the rest of the people bowed down upon their knees to drink water. And the Lord said unto Gideon, By the three hundred men that lapped will I save you, and deliver the Midianites into thine hand: and let all the other people go every man unto his place (Judges 7:5-7).

This is the difficult group. The other group left of their own free will when given the opportunity. This group will have to be told to leave. You had better prepare yourself, because this may not be easy. These people have been on the train a while. They have seen a few days with you. These may be very close friends. They may even be family members. Yes, I said family members. God is no respecter of persons when it comes to purpose. The Lord recognizes that they are not contributing, so they can only be receiving. You need people who can put something into you.

I know that they've been with you for years, but the question is, "Are they a part of God's purpose for your life?" Everybody you meet may not possess a substance that needs to be deposited into your life. Anyone who is depleting you and not making a corresponding deposit back into you is not a part of God's will for your life! God does not send people to take! Why? Because you're the promise. If you're the promise, God will send people to administer help to the promise!

Popularity or Purpose?

Today people in ministry are classified as "superstars." We've developed an arena for Christian idols. Our singers and psalmists seek the fame of Madonna and Michael Jackson. Our preachers have more bodyguards than presidents. We have sought to duplicate the world instead of the world duplicating us. We no longer hear the message of the songs. We no longer hear the cry of the preached Word. We are more excited by having someone's signature on our books.

Why can't everyone ride? Imagine seeing a train pull up at your stop. From the platform, you can see the cars are filled with some of the most notable names in the Christian arena today. The door opens, and the conductor asks you to get on.

Wouldn't you want to get on? That's the popular thing to do. Not everyone can ride on this train. Why not? Because the thing that determines a safe and successful ride is not the passengers but the *purpose*.

What is the purpose of the person in your life? You must judge the purpose and the motive for them being in your life. Are they moving you toward your divine destiny, or are they destroying something that God has for you?

You don't need friends in this hour. You may not like what I'm saying, but it's the truth. You don't need friends; you need covenant! This one verse conveys the essence of covenant:

> Greater love hath no man than this, that a man lay down his life for his friends (John 15:13).

Jesus referred to covenant when He used the term friend. He was not talking about the casual relationships that we call friendships. Most of you think that you have true friends when you have associates. True friends, according to Jesus, are people who are willing to give themselves up for you. That's covenant. My life for your life. My car for your car. A covenant relationship is unconditional. I don't need you to have an attitude every time I disagree with you. You can disagree and still be friends.

These people have purpose. They deposit into you as much as you deposit into them. These are the kinds of people that I need on my train. Even when I want to get off track, they will tell me the truth and help me stay on the right course.

Someone is hurting right now because a friend walked out on you. But were they really a friend? A covenant person never walks out. The relationship is stronger than death. Even after a person dies, you still keep up your part of the relationship with the family. God says, "I am giving you and have given you covenant."

> I the Lord have called thee in righteousness, and will hold thine hand, and will keep thee, and will give thee for a covenant of the people, for a light of the Gentiles (Isaiah 42:6).

This means that the person whom God sends will be there through the storm and the rain. They're going to be with me whether they like what I'm doing or not. Why? Because this person has been commissioned by God to assist me on this train ride. I don't have time to be bothered with people whom God hasn't sent my way.

I don't care how nice you are. I don't care how famous you are. I don't care what you have. This is the issue: Did God send you my way? Are you the person that God has attached to my life to cause me to reach my destination? Reaching my goal is the only goal on my mind. I have to stay on the train to reach my goal.

Chapter 7

Sister to Sister

I want to have a heart-to-heart talk with my single sisters. Many of you are questioning God about when He's going to send you the right man. You may even think you have the right one now, but one question lingers in your mind.

"What if this isn't God?"

Let's have a sister to sister talk.

Before you go where God intends you to go, or have what God intends you to have, you must get your priorities in order. God will never give you anything that will not enhance your life. He is not about replacing Himself. If you put God in the right position, God will give you something that is unforgettable.

Let's look at a woman who had her priorities in order.

Then took Mary a pound of ointment of spikenard, very costly, and anointed the feet of Jesus, and wiped his feet with her hair: and the house was filled with the odour of ointment (John 12:3).

You have to be complete within yourself before anything can be added. Mary wasn't concerned about a husband. She was seeking only one person—Jesus! Many other men sat in that room, but the only person that mattered was Jesus.

Sister, the best way to get to your man is to get to Jesus.

Seek ye first the kingdom of God, and his righteousness; and all these things shall be added unto you (Matthew 6:33).

A High Price

Mary used something she cherished to minister to Jesus. She was willing to pay a high price to reach her prize.

Spikenard, a very expensive ointment, was used as a healing agent. She took something that was valuable, that could actually bring healing to her, and poured it out on the Lord. She willingly sacrificed to show Jesus the passion she had for Him. Sometimes we have to experience pain to get to Jesus.

In fact, Mary didn't let anything deter her from her mission. Not the others in the room. Not the scorn she might receive. Not the gossip she might hear. She pressed through it all.

Can God find a woman who is obsessed with getting to the feet of Jesus? A sister who is so crazy about praising and worshiping God that she doesn't even notice Mr. Right when he comes into the room? A sister whose passion is for the presence of God?

Only One Master

God isn't going to give you Mr. Right if he's going to divert your attention every time you get ready to do something for the Lord. Why would God give up His throne in your life for a man? Honey, you serve a jealous God Who, is not about to share you with anyone.

This is one of the major problems with single women who are looking for a man. You can serve only one master. When a man gives you some attention, you try to divide your worship. You are looking for another King.

Mary had only one object of her desire. She was not concerned about what people might say. She was not concerned with how the men in the room viewed her. She did not care about her reputation. She just wanted to get to Jesus.

Mary wanted to minister to her Master. She wanted to give Him an unforgettable experience. Her worship said, "If I never see You again, You will never forget this night. I am going to do for You what no one has ever done. I am going to show You how much I really love You. I will even let down my hair and give You everything I've got."

The apostle Paul wrote that a woman's hair is her glory. (See 1 Cor. 11:15.) This woman gave her glory to worship Jesus. She gave up prestige and honor to show that nothing she had was too good for her Lord. This kind of worship provokes a response from God. The Lord could not sit still during all of this attention. He had to let the world know what she did for Him.

A Woman God Can Bless

This is the kind of woman whom the Lord can bless. He will give her not only a man but every desire of her heart. She is not serving the Lord *until* He gives her a man. She is not serving the Lord *to get* a man. She doesn't come to church looking for anyone besides Jesus. When she does her hair, it's to look good for Jesus. When she puts on her make-up, she has Jesus in mind. She aims to go to church to give Him everything she has. She has decided, "Even if He doesn't bless me with a man, I'm satisfied with my Master." Imagine that.

Jesus was so mesmerized by her worship that He interrupted His message and noticed this woman. Her praise was so powerful that she actually made Jesus pause in the middle of speaking. Imagine how awesome her worship had to be! Jesus lost His train of thought for a moment and focused on this woman.

Jesus was so impressed that He made people stop talking about her. He wouldn't let anyone else touch her. Jesus came to the woman's defense and said, "Leave her alone."

The Lord will not forget your labor of love. When your motives are right, Jesus will reward you openly. Jesus told the crowd who witnessed her extravagance:

> For in that she hath poured this ointment on my body, she did it for my burial. Verily I say unto you, Wheresoever this gospel shall be preached in the whole world, there shall also this, that this woman hath done, be told for a memorial of her (Matthew 26:12,13).

Did you catch the most powerful thing about the entire incident? Jesus declared that everyone who attempted to preach Him would have to mention her. This event found its way into the gospel and is preached to this day.

Pour It Out

The Lord said, "She hath poured this ointment on my body." Sister, that's a powerful statement. She took what she had and poured it out on the body of Christ. She decided that her anointing would not be wasted. Are you willing to pour out your anointing on the body of Christ?

This ointment represented what she had stored and hid from others. She sealed precious things into a box so that they could be protected. Many of you have sealed up your anointing, trying to protect it from others. The Lord says to you, "Pour out your oil upon the body. Anoint another sister with your oil. Release what you've been reserving for some future time."

Because this woman broke her alabaster box and let others see and smell what she had been hiding, Jesus set up a memorial for her. He gave her something that she would never forget. He gave her something she did not even ask for.

Look a little closer at what Jesus said. He told every preacher in the room to preach what this woman did.

What did she do? She provoked a blessing through her worship. She did not worship to get a blessing, but she worshiped and received a blessing. Herein lies the key to receiving from God. You have to forget about yourself and your needs and start meeting the needs of someone else.

Worship God by serving His body. Anoint the body of Christ with your experience, and watch God move on your behalf. Pour out what you treasure on the body, and see God pour you out a blessing that you don't have room to receive.

One Seat Beside You

I sense some women saying, "God, if You don't send me a husband, I can't make it."

Yes, you can make it because you're in the ark of safety.

I know what you're feeling. Trust me, you would rather have nothing than to have what doesn't belong to you. When people say, "It doesn't look like you're ever going to get married," tell them, "I'm on a train, and my husband stop has not come yet."

What is God saying?

"I haven't forsaken you, but you have to wait until your train gets to this stop. Go ahead and buy a house because that's your next stop. Stop questioning Me about a husband, because I've got a stop called Husband. Just ride the train until you get there."

God will permit only those people who will minister to you to board the train. They're going to ride with you only a certain number of miles, and then God's going to move them. He's going to put other people on, and they're going to get to certain stops and tell you, "This is my stop, and I've got to get off!"

Many of you don't understand why some of your closest friends are fading out. Listen, you can't get frustrated. You can't shed tears about it. Why? Because they have ridden the miles of your life that were predestined by God. When their term is up because they've completed the job that God gave them to do, then let them off. Stop holding on to people. Let them go! Tell them, "I understand because I have to release you."

There is only one other seat besides yours. Listen to me and understand the danger in allowing another person to occupy that seat too long. If you don't let this person off when the time comes to let her off, when you get to the depot that's marked Husband, there will not be a seat.

"But that's my best girlfriend sitting in that seat. Honey, we are going to be friends until we die."

Sister, I don't think you heard me. Your man is outside waiting to get on the train. Now what are you going to do? Are you going to let Jackie keep sitting there? Whom do you want? It's time for her to get up because there's only one seat.

You Determine the Speed

Sister, if you're single, God is going to anoint you for celibacy. No one can touch you, or even hug you, because when your husband comes to get on the train, he will be looking for an undefiled temple.

He can see all fingerprints that are not his because God is going to give him X-ray vision. He is going to say, "Well, I think I see some prints over here somewhere. Where else did this train stop? Who else has been on this train?"

Do you understand what this means? This means the man can't feel me. He can't touch me. He can't rub me. He can't kiss me. From this day forward, every time you allow it, the train pauses outside the depot for about 30 minutes. Thirty minutes in the sight of God can be three years.

The length of time required for you to get to the promises of God in your life depends upon you not holding up the train. You govern the speed. If you want a 40 mile per hour train, just let God's ordained people get on.

"When am I going to get married, Lord?" The Lord says, "You tell Me!"

Am I going to get married? Are you? You tell God how fast to go by the way you live.

Somebody told me, "Sister Juanita, if I didn't know better, I would think you were a virgin. I said, "I am, because I'm clean. My hands are holy! They have not been down any zippers. They are holy!" Because God is holy, He requires us to be holy too.

> For I am the Lord your God: ye shall therefore sanctify yourselves, and ye shall be holy; for I am holy: neither shall ye defile yourselves with any manner of creeping thing that creepeth upon the earth. For I am the Lord that bringeth you up out of the land of Egypt, to be your God: ye shall therefore be holy, for I am holy (Leviticus 11:44,45).

After my divorce, God touched me and healed my brokenness. I believe He restored everything that I lost during that devastating time. I consider myself a spiritual virgin. If God ever leads me into marriage, I want to obey Him every step of the way.

Your Soul Mate

God is raising up sisters who will choose men in the Spirit. Some of you have been dating men who will choose somebody else. You're going to think that woman is so ugly. Why? Because you are not more clean than she is.

Your hair is longer than hers and she has a wet Gheri Curl, but she was to his satisfaction. How? She did something for his spirit. What can you do for his spirit? You are supposed to be his helpmeet. He does not need you to help him be a man. He needs you to help him be a spiritual man.

What can you and he do together for the kingdom? He doesn't need a woman with big legs or long hair or a weave. If her spirit is pure and she motivates the God in him, she becomes his soul mate.

God is searching for your soul mate. The right man in your life is your soul mate. He's the thing that makes your anointing come alive. If you're with somebody right now and he isn't motivating the anointing in you, he isn't your soul mate.

He's your boyfriend, lover, or man, but he isn't the other connection to your soul. He isn't the heartbeat to your spirit. He doesn't drive the blood through your spiritual veins. He does nothing but motivate your flesh and entice you to sin.

Someone once told me that I was losing weight. I told them that I was really losing weight–the weight and the sin that so easily besets me. (See Hebrews 12:1.) I want to be chosen. I don't want to run after a man. I want a man with whom I can live the rest of my days. When we have done all we can do in this life, I will see him again in another life. We will never die! Love never dies!

The Bible says, "Whoso findeth a wife findeth a good thing, and obtaineth favour of the Lord" (Proverbs 18:22). That's why some of you don't have the favor of God on your marriage! It's only when he finds, and not when she finds.

Guess what?

The choice is not up to you. God gives the man the power to choose. If he is sold out to God and living uprightly before Him, God will honor his request.

You may have said, "I'll never marry a fat man in my life!" One day you may walk in church and say, "I think I like that fat man."

Do you know why? Because God has given him favor. He's making you like what He's about to do.

I used to tell God I want him to be tall and dark. I want him to have a mustache and wear a certain suit, shoes, etc.

Now, my spirit says, "God, I don't care what he looks like. Just bring him."

I'm not picky now! If he has a polyester suit, I will dress him up. If he is fat, I will help him lose weight. If he is white, I will help him get a tan. Just send him!

Lose your ideas. God is going to give you what you need. Make a vow to the Lord. "No man will handle me unless he is my husband. No man will touch me, rub me, feel me, unless he is my husband. My life is off limits! I am on this train to stay!"

Chapter 8

Who Called You?

The most precious commodity in the whole world is a word from the Lord. Many people seek things, but all I need is to hear the Lord's voice. I'm like Job:

I have esteemed the words of his mouth more than my necessary food (Job 23:12b).

We need this attitude to stay on the train. Do you consider the Word of God to be nothing less than the breath of life? Without His Word, I would die.

Life on the train is synonymous with life in the Word. You must stay in the Word of God to stay on the train. Jesus taught us about the connection between the truth and staying free.

Then said Jesus to those Jews which believed on him, If ye continue in my word, then are ye my disciples indeed; and ye shall know the truth, and the truth shall make you free (John 8:31,32).

Did you catch that? If you continue in the Word, you will be disciplined enough to know it. He did not say, "If ye get a dose of the Word." He said, "If ye continue." That means to constantly go after more of God. Sunday morning Christians get only a dose, and that's why there are so many people in bondage. You are in bondage to flesh. You are in bondage to tradition. You are even in bondage to self-righteousness. Look at Scripture carefully.

If you're consistently in the Word of God, you'll recognize it when you hear it. You won't be tossed about by every wind of doctrine. You won't be easily influenced by the wrong thing. When someone tells you something that doesn't line up with the Word of God, you dismiss it instead of falling prey to it. So many people are misled by unfounded prophecies.

These so-called prophecies have caused us to lose our focus. You don't even know what you were born to do. You don't even know what you have become.

Parking Lot Prophecies

Some of you are living on a couple of parking lot prophecies. You leave the parking lot thinking that you're anointed for a particular job, but all you have is an emotional word from the mouth of a cheap imitation of the real thing.

What did the apostle Paul say about that kind of anointing and how you really get it?

> Neglect not the gift that is in thee, which was given thee by prophecy, with the laying on of the hands of the presbytery. Meditate upon these things; give thyself wholly to them; that thy profiting may appear to all (1 Timothy 4:14,15).

That means proven prophecies. When you meet people who claim to speak for God, find out if they've been tested and proven. Seasoned saints have something to impart to your life. A true prophet brings a life-changing experience with him.

Sadly, many of you are functioning off these closed-door prophecies. You have come out of a church bathroom and declared that you are called of God. I'm not trying to offend you; I'm trying to help you. You may be called, but God doesn't have to call you behind closed doors. If you are truly called, then there should be some signs.

Sister so-and-so may have told you that God called you to be something. Have you built a train without waiting on God? Does the evidence show that you're profiting in your calling? According to the last phrase in the above Scripture, Paul told Timothy that his profiting would be evident to everyone.

Confirm Your Calling

The first thing we must deal with is the calling. You've been called. So what? Does that really mean anything? The Lord himself addressed that issue.

> So the last shall be first, and the first last: for many be called, but few chosen (Matthew 20:16).

Those are not my words. Jesus Himself said that! Many people have a call on their life, but only a few will actually accomplish what God has called them to do. The Bible says that "the gifts and calling of God are without repentance" (Romans 11:29).

What does that mean? Many drunks and drug addicts are called, but they may never enter the realm of the chosen. If you went to the cemetery, you could probably find many graves of people who were called but never produced. It's not about what Prophet or Prophetess Smith says. It's about what God said.

> Then the word of the Lord came unto me, saying, Before I formed thee in the belly I knew thee; and before thou cameth forth out of the womb I sanctified thee, and I ordained thee a prophet unto the nations (Jeremiah 1:4,5).

That clarifies the point. The Lord told Jeremiah that not only did He know him, but before he was even born He sanctified him. What does sanctify mean? That means He set him apart or chose him. The Lord said, "Not only did I call you, but I chose you. Not only did I choose you, but I ordained or approved you to do the work that I have called you to do. I put you on the train, and stamped your ticket *approved* from Heaven."

What Are You Producing?

How can you tell if you have a genuine call on your life? The answers to your questions can be easily determined by a little fruit inspection.

> Ye have not chosen me, but I have chosen you, and ordained you, that you should go and bring forth fruit, and that your fruit should remain: that whatsoever ye shall ask of the Father in my name, he may give it you (John 15:16).

You've laid your own tracks, and you're making a mess across the country. Everything that you touch turns sour. Everything you try to do fails. You get no recognition. You get no honor. You have no glory. The evidence says you're not on God's train. You're on a man-made train. You've gotten off God's train and headed down the wrong track on your own train. Get back on track by returning to the Word of God. Commit your life to God, not to your own agenda, and watch Him put you back on the right track.

I beseech ye therefore, brethren, by the mercies of God, that ye present your bodies a living sacrifice, holy, acceptable unto God, which is your reasonable service. And be not conformed to this world: but be ye transformed by the renewing of your mind, that ye may prove what is that good, and acceptable, and perfect, will of God (Romans 12:1,2).

Give God your undivided attention. Disregard what you thought and find out the truth. Do that which is right in the sight of God. Stop trying to bless yourself. Stop trying to promote yourself. Just devote your whole heart to God. Engulf yourself in the Word of God until your way of thinking lines up with His. By doing this, you can judge your prophecy. Prove it next to the Word to know if it is that "good, and acceptable, and perfect will of God" for your life. God wants you to stay on the train and stop only where He directs you.

Confusing Voices

Imagine a train of box cars from the early 1900s. The conductor wore a hat and a navy jacket. The box car assistants wore crisp white jackets with hats that buckled beneath their chin. These assistants had a level of superiority over the people, but they were not the conductor.

Don't ever get the voice of the Conductor confused with the voice of the assistant. An assistant only helps you with instructions from the Conductor. The assistant does not tell you where to go nor what to do apart from the Conductor.

Let's carry the analogy into the Christian arena. The Conductor is the voice of the shepherd. Evangelists, missionaries, teachers, and prophets in the body of Christ will confirm what the shepherd already knows to be true in the direct path of a person's life. Anyone coming to prophesy something contrary is out of line.

The Conductor is the shepherd. He has followed you from the time you got on the train. He knows you by name. By now, the Conductor is very familiar with your face. He's seen your smile. He knows your pattern.

Listen carefully.

If a good pastor is walking with you for any amount of years, he knows what you can handle. He knows what you are ready for. He also knows what you're not ready for. He seats you according to what he knows you can handle.

Some people can't handle sunlight. Some people have to eat every two hours because they're diabetic. The Conductor has all the instructions for each of the passengers on the train. He watches to make sure someone doesn't hand a diabetic a plate of sugar cookies. He knows the diabetic can't handle too much sugar. Your Conductor knows what your spiritual body can digest.

Beware of the assassin assigned by the enemy. These people will cloak themselves with a garment and a title only to deceive you.

Assistants prophesy to you to ignite the part of your flesh that God wants to kill. They want to cloak you with something that God wants to remove. The Lord wants you to die to the flesh. He wants you to die to wanting to be seen. The assistants say feed the flesh, while the Lord says kill the flesh.

They come to feed your ego. They want to feed the ministry part of you while the Conductor wants to assist you to make sure you get to that destination safely. Those assistants become a hazard to your life. They whisper thoughts of getting off the train. They make you think that someone is holding you back against your own will. They tell you that the train is going too slow for you and you had better get off.

This individual's instructions are contrary to the teaching of the shepherd. That's why you need to beware of parking lot prophecies. Anybody who prophesies into your life should only confirm what God has already spoken to you.

My Train Moved On

I got off the train at Port Huron. Everyone who came into my church called me out and said that God was going to raise me up. I began to receive parking lot prophecies of people telling me that I should not be there.

I ran away. I left my clothes and everything and went back to Chicago to my parents' home. I jumped off the train. Therefore, my ears were beyond the reach of the Conductor's voice. I could no longer hear Him calling me back to safety. When the train stopped, there were messages throughout the depot, but I was not there to receive the calls telling Juanita Bynum to report to the first box car because the train was about to take off. I was running in the opposite direction. I was running toward what I thought was my final destination. I ran into a bad situation. My story is in the book, *No More Sheets*.

I never should have gotten into an awful relationship. Finally, like the prodigal son, I came to myself. I realized I was right in the gutter of life.

I had to get back on the train, but how? I felt emotionally damaged. My ticket had been torn up. The train had moved on. How could I return to make it right?

Finally, I realized the train is a spiritual thing. You may miss it in the natural, but you can go back in the spirit and regain all that you have lost.

I picked up the phone and called my former pastor and repented to him and his wife. I said to them, "I am under a curse. Nothing will ever go right for me until you forgive me and then bless me. I need you to cover me until the train comes back again."

This time it was a spiritual covering. I was willing to stand there as long as it took until the next train came by. The train came in the form of PanAmerica Airlines. It took me to New York City where I walked in a church.

I remember driving down the street after six months in New York. I used to hear a church on the radio. I was being ministered to by this particular pastor. On my way to work at 7:00 a.m., I saw a lady at the bus stop. (Now I could hear the voice of the Conductor when He spoke because I was going in the right direction.)

The Lord told me to give the lady a ride to church. When we arrived, she invited me in. Within 30 minutes, the pastor began to preach. He looked out at me and told me I was like an eagle with broken wings, but God had a ministry in me. He said my worst days were behind me and my best days were yet to come. He continued to say that God was going to raise me up. When I came to, I was picking myself up from between the seats. I knew that I had been reconnected with a new conductor.

Back to the Beginning

You pay a price for getting off the train. You have to go all the way around the route again and again as from the beginning.

I found myself back in the projects, shaking roaches out of my clothes. I found myself having to trust God for food again. I found myself being poor and without again. I had to go to McDonald's (drive-thru) to get extra napkins so that I could have toilet paper.

I had to repeat the ride all over again, but this time I was determined not to get off the train. I found myself again sitting on the front row and being the pastor's intercessor. I found myself once more having to take rebuke. I had to be reproved and instructed, but this time I was determined not to get off the train.

I found myself again being approached by the voice of God, saying, "Will you come work for Me? Can I use you?" I shut myself in and went on long fasts. I spent much time in prayer, but this time I was determined not to get off the train.

Finally, in September 1996, my stop came. I had waited for it for years. But this time, I was ready. I wasn't going to miss my destiny. God divinely orchestrated my circumstances, allowing me to minister at Bishop T. D. Jakes' "Woman Thou Art Loosed" conference.

The Lord declared that it was my time to reach people. It's as if He said, "I buried her beneath some things until I got ready to put the spotlight on her. She's gone through enough to help somebody. Her time is at hand. Turn the spotlight on Bynum. I've put something fresh and revolutionary in her. It took some pain and the passing of time, but she's on track. My daughter is ready now."

I got off the train because I knew that was my divine stop. How? When you're embarrassed by the masses, you're at the right stop. When your way is already made, you're at the right stop. When your blessings are already before you, you're at the right stop. When people are standing at the depot to sow into your life and bless you, you're at the right stop. When encouragement is waiting, you're at the right stop.

When you get off at the right destination, you're on the ground. You're not high-minded. Popularity doesn't mean anything. You can embrace the blessings of the stop, but you don't change the depth of your relationship with the Conductor. You've reached your divine destination.

No matter what you're going through, hold on. A divine destiny awaits you. It will fulfill you like nothing else. It's the very reason why Jesus Christ apprehended you. It's yours for the taking.

You need to do only one thing: *Don't get off the train!*

About the Author

Prophetess Juanita Bynum is the president and founder of Juanita Bynum Ministries in Hempstead, New York. Her anointed messages of healing and deliverance is demanding a global spotlight that is transcending cultural and denominational boundaries. She flows under a powerful threefold prophetic, evangelistic and psalmist anointing which manifest spiritual breakthrough throughout America and other countries around the world. She has also appeared as a guest speaker on multiple television and radio programs. Prophetess Bynum is the host of the successful annual "Women: Weapons of Power" conference.

Other Products by Juanita Bynum

Books

The Planted Seed
The Immutable Laws of Sowing and Reaping

This book contains remarkable insights about the most valuable gems you possess–your seed. Do you realize the potential impact your seed has to produce extraordinary results in the realm of the spirit and the magnitude of responsibility you have as a sower of your seed? Allow the powerful truth of this book to penetrate deep into your heart to bring you to a high level of understanding of the unique biblical principle of sowing and reaping.

No More Sheets!
Wholeness through Holiness

There has never been a more needed message to reach people who have suffered with their ability to maintain virtuous relationships. Many sincere, well-meaning Christians secretly wrestle with their sexuality and lust. This personal issue has trapped many of us, but God longs to heal what we've been afraid to reveal. Juanita Bynum pulls the covers off this powerful struggle. This message is your breakthrough to wholeness and holiness.

Cassettes

No More Sheets!
Don't Get Off the Train
My Inheritance
Integrity
Never Mess with a Man Who Came Out of a Cave
A Place Called There
Singles, It's Your Time
Second Decision
I Apologize
Praise & Worship

Videos

No More Sheets!
The Spirit of Isaac
Morning Glory I & II
Loosing the Anointing